CW00736031

FIELD NOTES ON SURVIVAL

Amy Acre is the editor of Bad Betty Press and the author of two PBS Choice pamphlets, *And They Are Covered in Gold Light* (Bad Betty) and *Where We're Going, We Don't Need Roads* (flipped eye). Her poem 'every girl knows' won the 2019 Verve Poetry Prize.

Jake Wild Hall is one half of Bad Betty Press, and the winner of the PBH 2016 Spirit Of The Free Fringe Award. He is the author of two pamphlets, *Blank* and *Solomon's World*—longlisted for Best Pamphlet in the 2018 Saboteur Awards. He co-edited anthologies *The Dizziness of Freedom* and *Alter Egos*.

Rachel Long is a poet and the founder of Octavia Poetry Collective for Womxn of Colour. Rachel's poetry and prose have been published widely, most recently in *Mal*, *Granta* and *The Poetry Review*. She is assistant tutor on the Barbican Young Poets programme. Her Forward Prize-nominated debut collection, *My Darling from the Lions*, was published by Picador in August 2020.

Sarah Aluko is a Nigerian-British author and poet. Her poetry speaks of womanhood, being black, love and loss. In 2017, she released her collection, *Firstborn*. Sarah has been longlisted for the Outspoken Poetry Prize two years in a row and was listed as part of Nasty Boy's Creative Class of 2018, which was featured in *Okay Africa*, *Marie Claire*, *Dazed* and *Hunger Magazine*. Sarah was a speaker at TEDx Tottenham in April 2019, sharing her journey on becoming an author.

Mandisa Apena is a cancer sun and part time vegan from South London. They are an interdisciplinary artist interested in ecology, dreams and post-apocalyptic cannibalism. They are a Barbican Young Poet alumni, member of London Queer Writers, host of occasional queer poetry night: 'hot 4 u' and author of self-published poetry book *and twice as bitter*.

Dean Atta's debut poetry collection, *I Am Nobody's Nigger*, was shortlisted for the Polari First Book Prize. His novel in verse, *The Black Flamingo*, won the 2020 Stonewall Book Award and was shortlisted for the CILIP Carnegie Medal, YA Book Prize and Jhalak Prize.

Khairani Barokka is an Indonesian writer, artist, and translator in London, whose work has been presented extensively, in fifteen countries. She was *Modern Poetry in Translation*'s Inaugural Poet-In-Residence, and is Researcher-in-Residence at UAL's Decolonising the Arts Institute. Among Okka's honours, she was an NYU Tisch Departmental Fellow and is a UNFPA Indonesian Young Leader Driving Social Change. Okka is co-editor of *STAIRS AND WHISPERS: D/dEAF AND DISABLED POETS WRITE BACK* (Nine Arches Press), author-illustrator of *INDIGENOUS SPECIES* (Tilted Axis; Vietnamese translation published by AJAR Press), and author of debut poetry collection *ROPE* (Nine Arches).

Jeremiah Brown is a Black British-Jamaican writer and performer based in Croydon. He's a Barbican Young Poet alumni and former Roundhouse resident artist. His debut solo show *Likkle Rum with Grandma* is a journey of mortality, migration and identity. Jeremiah's commissions include Nationwide Building Society, St Paul's Cathedral, Barbican and The Poetry Society.

Claire Collison is a cross-disciplinary artist, and was an honouree of the inaugural Women Poets' Prize. Her poems have been placed in various prizes, and can be found in *The Rialto*, *The Valley Press Anthology of Prose Poetry*, *Butcher's Dog*, *Perverse*, *Magma*, *Corrupted Poets*, and *Finished Creatures*. clairecollison.com

Courtney Conrad is a Jamaican poet. She was the Roundhouse Poetry Slam runner-up in 2018. She is a Roundhouse Poetry Collective, BBC Words First and Poet in the City Producer alumni. She has competed internationally at CUPSI 2018 in Philadelphia. She has been a featured poet at Glastonbury Festival and the UKYA Festival in 2019. She is also a BBC Fringe Slam finalist. Her poetry explores the intersectionality between Black, Caribbean, Queer, Christian and Womxn identities.

Zad El Bacha's work combines political and community building experience with Middle-Eastern poetic traditions to write on migration, sexual trauma, and sexual and gender identity. Zad won a 2019/2020 London Writers Award, and Italy's biggest poetry slam, PoverArte. Zad has written on migration and colonialism for VICE and Red Pepper and recently published a pamphlet with the Italian cultural magazine *inutile*. Zad is the co-founder of Coriander, a theatre collective for queer artists of colour, and has written theatre shows preserving her oral family histories of war and migration for the Camden People's Theatre and the North Wall.

Chloe Elliott is a British / Malaysian-Chinese poet based in Durham where she is currently studying English Literature. There she is President of the Poetry Society and helps facilitate workshops and run spoken-word events. She is the winner of the 2019 Timothy Corsellis Prize and a 2020 Creative Future Writers' Award, and is a member of the Writing Squad.

Maia Elsner grew up between Oxford and Mexico City, and has Mexican and Polish Jewish heritage. She was shortlisted for the 2020 Mairtin Crawford Award for Poetry and commended for the 2020 Geoff Stevens Memorial Award. Her poems have been published in *Magma, Colorado Review, Wildness, The Missouri Review* and others.

Sarah Fletcher is an American-British writer. Her poems have been published in *Poetry London, The White Review, The Rialto* and more. Her third pamphlet, *Caviar*, is upcoming from Out-Spoken Press in 2020. She is currently working towards her debut collection.

Kat François is a former BBC3, UK and World Slam Champion. A performance artist, director, youth facilitator and personal trainer, Kat runs a young people's writing and performance collective. She regularly appears in national media, and her acclaimed one woman play, *Raising Lazarus*, on the history of Caribbean soldiers in World War One, has toured internationally.

Kathryn Hargett is an undergraduate at the University of Alabama at Birmingham. A 2018 Best New Poet, she is the recipient of fellowships from Kundiman, Belgrade Art Studio, and the University of Alabama at Birmingham. Most recently, she received the Barksdale-Maynard Prize in Poetry and was selected as a National YoungArts Foundation Finalist in Writing. She is editor-in-chief of *TRACK//FOUR* and on staff at *Winter Tangerine*. Find her in *Best New Poets, BARNHOUSE, Anomaly, The Adroit Journal, The Miami Rail, Tinderbox Poetry Journal*, and elsewhere.

Kirsten Irving is a Lincs-born, London-based poet, editor and voiceover, and one half of the team behind collaborative poetry press Sidekick Books. Her work has been published by Salt and Happenstance, widely anthologised, awarded the Live Canon prize and thrown out of a helicopter. Were she in Battle Royale, she would love to be Takako Chigusa but really she'd be a total Yuko Sakaki. @KoftheTriffids www.kirstenirving.com

Emma Jeremy was born in Bristol and lives in London. Her poems have featured in *Poetry London, Magma, Rising* and *Poems in Which*. In 2018 she won the New Poets Prize, and her debut pamphlet *Safety Behaviour* was published by Smith|Doorstop in 2019.

Safiya Kamaria Kinshasa is a British-born Barbadian-raised multidisciplinary poet. She is a recipient of the Jerwood Arts | Apples & Snakes Poetry in Performance Programme, the winner of the 2020 New Voice in Poetry Prize and was shortlisted for the Out-Spoken Page Poetry Prize. Her work has appeared in *The Caribbean Writer, The Amistad, Alter Egos* (Bad Betty Press) and more.

Anja Konig grew up in the German language and now writes in English. Her pamphlet *Advice for an Only Child* was shortlisted for the 2015 Michael Marks prize. Her first collection *Animal Experiments* (Bad Betty Press) was *The Telegraph*'s Poetry Book of the Month.

Christopher Lanyon is a poet, mathematician and PhD student based in Nottingham, UK. His poems have been published in *Abridged, Strix, Finished Creatures* and Bad Betty Press's *Alter Egos* anthology, among others.

Billie Manning is a teacher and poet from Hackney. Having grown up writing, she eventually graduated from teenage Harry Potter erotica to poetry that has nothing to do with puns on the word 'wand'. She teaches poetry courses at City Lit and is a Barbican Young Poet 2020.

Arji Manuelpillai is a poet, performer and creative facilitator based in London. For over 15 years Arji has worked with community arts projects nationally and internationally. Recently, his poetry has been published by magazines including *Prole, Cannon's Mouth, Strix, The Rialto* and *The Lighthouse Journal*. He has also been shortlisted for the BAME Burning Eye pamphlet prize 2018, The Robert Graves Prize 2018, The Oxford Prize 2019 and The Live Canon Prize. Arji is a member of Wayne Holloway-Smith's poetry group, Malika's Poetry Kitchen and London Stanza. Arji's debut pamphlet *Mutton Rolls* was published with Out-Spoken Press. www.arji.org

Alex Mazey (b.1991) won The Roy Fisher Prize for Poetry. He was also the recipient of a Creative Future Writers' Award in 2019. His poetry has featured in anthologies and literary press magazines, most notably in *The London Magazine*. His collection of essays, *Living in Disneyland*, will be available from Broken Sleep Books in October 2020.

Jenny Mitchell is joint winner of the Geoff Stevens' Memorial Poetry Prize 2019, and winner of the Fosseway Poetry Competition 2020. She's been published in *The Rialto*, *The Interpreter's House* and *Under the Radar* etc. A debut collection, *Her Lost Language* (Indigo Dreams) was selected as one of the 44 Poetry Books of 2019 (Poetry Wales).

Jess Murrain is an inter-disciplinary creative working mainly as an actor and theatre-maker. Her poetry appears in *Under the Radar* and *Tentacular* and her wider practice includes artist moving image and film poetry. She is co-founder of Theatre with Legs, an experimental devised theatre company. She lives in London.

André Naffis-Sahely is the author of *The Promised Land: Poems from Itinerant Life* (Penguin, 2017) and *The Other Side of Nowhere* (Rough Trade Books, 2019), as well as the editor of *The Heart of a Stranger: An Anthology of Exile Literature* (Pushkin Press, 2020).

Gboyega Odubanjo is a British-Nigerian poet born and raised in East London. In 2018 he completed an MA in Poetry at the University of East Anglia. His pamphlet *While I Yet Live* was published by Bad Betty Press in 2019. In 2020 he won the New Poets Prize. He is a member of the Barbican Young Poets, the Roundhouse Poetry Collective, and (In)Space.

Jacqueline Saphra's collection *All My Mad Mothers* was shortlisted for the 2017 T.S. Eliot prize. It was followed by *Dad, Remember You are Dead* in 2019, both from Nine Arches Press. *A Bargain with the Light: Poems after Lee Miller* (2017) and *Veritas: Poems after Artemisia* (2020) are both published by Hercules Editions.

Tom Sastry's collection *A Man's House Catches Fire* (Nine Arches Press, 2019) was shortlisted for the 2020 Seamus Heaney First Collection Prize. His pamphlet, *Complicity* (Smith/Doorstop 2016), was a Poetry School Book of the Year and a Poetry Book Society pamphlet choice.

Anna Walsh is an Irish writer based in Glasgow. They have had poetry and prose published in *Fallow Media, Spamzine*, and *The Stinging Fly*, among others. They have work forthcoming in anthologies with Monstrous Regiment Publishing and 3ofCups Press. They are currently working on a short story collection.

Antosh Wojcik is a poet, drummer and sound artist. His solo performance piece, *How To Keep Time: A Drum Solo for Dementia* explores vascular dementia through drumming and spoken word. It was produced by Penned In The Margins and toured the UK and internationally throughout 2019 with support from Arts Council England.

Liv Wynter is a support worker, live artist, writer, and activist from SEL. Liv has been performing internationally since 2015, making live art that centres around radical action, community, rage, and power. Quit your job, join a band, start a gang.

Field Notes on Survival

Published by Bad Betty Press in 2020
www.badbettypress.com

The rights of Amy Acre and Jake Wild Hall to be identified as the editors of this work has been asserted by them in accordance with Section 77 of the Copyright, Designs and Patents Act of 1988.

Cover photography by Amaal Said, Jamie Cameron, Holly Whitaker, Derrick Kakembo, Ruth Crafer, Thomas Sammut, Naomi Woddis, Sloetry Photography, Henry Harrison and Martin Brown

Printed and bound in the United Kingdom

A CIP record of this book is available from the British Library.

ISBN: 978-1-913268-12-1

LOTTERY FUNDED

Supported using public funding by

ARTS COUNCIL ENGLAND

Field Notes on Survival

PRESS

A house is a home even when it's dark.

– Ben Harper

Field Notes on Survival

Edited by Amy Acre and Jake Wild Hall

In memory of Dean McKee

FIELD AGENT	PAPERS	PAGE
Rachel Long	Foreword	19

Unit 00001

Sarah Aluko	Club quarantine, no face mask, no entry	25
	On the internet	27
Mandisa Apena	Sacrificial Lamb	30
Dean Atta	Two Black Boys in Paradise	32
	Hip Hop Line Dancing in Dallas	34
Khairani Barokka	how to avoid one's self as a vulnerable person in a pandemic	35
	This past one year (2017)	36
	extraction rumination, in the words of the lithosphere	38
Jeremiah Brown	Rumour Has It	40
Claire Collison	Premonition	42
	The flag	43

Unit 00002

Courtney Conrad	Roadkill	47
Zad El Bacha	A coffee	48
	The streets in my fascist village	49
Chloe Elliott	eating orange peel is an act against god	51
Maia Elsner	Christmas in diaspora	52
Sarah Fletcher	On Babies	55
Kat François	Tone of Existence	56
	Light	57

Unit 00003

Kathryn Hargett	Sonnet Interrupted by a Gunshot	61
	No Hunting, No Trespassing	63
Kirsten Irving	House Arrest	65
	Self-Portrait as a Reality Show Character Arc	67
	They were my friends	68
Emma Jeremy	all i know is it tumbling out of me	70
	sorry	71
	it takes many people to prepare for a single death	72
Safiya Kamaria Kinshasa	The Inaugural Ball of Heresy	74
	Choose Your Quarantine House...	76
Anja Konig	Why Is This Night Different From All Other Nights?	79
Christopher Lanyon	landfill	80
	Time was a backward rote of names and mishaps	81
	Gannets	82

Unit 00004

Billie Manning	Spellwork	89
	before robbie overdoses alone in a house in the country	90
	in the dream I walk away from you without saying a word	94
Arji Manuelpillai	I love you	96
	look in the other direction	97
Alex Mazey	Kaczynski's Day	98
	Beneath Orange Mountain	100
Jenny Mitchell	Her Remains	101
	Mastering Her Landscape	102
Jess Murrain	Prince's Audition	103
	Dad Crouches Over His Insomnia	104
	One in Four Cowboys Were Black	105
André Naffis-Sahely	Wildfires	107

Unit 00005

| Gboyega Odubanjo | STICKS AND STONES | 111 |

Jacqueline Saphra   Seder Sonnet   112
Good Friday   113

Tom Sastry   Victoria   114
If you are reading this, I am still alive   115
Kathy Beale   116

Anna Walsh   A Faggot & Their Friend   118

Antosh Wojcik   Transaction Fees   120
Unanswered Calls on the Voicemail Machine of
Deleted Animé Character #53   121

Liv Wynter   122

Editors   Notes, acknowledgements and thanks   124

Foreword

I became aware that words 'survivor' and 'survival' were having a renaissance some five years ago at the inaugural Clear Lines Festival, founded by the incredible Winnie N Li and Dr Nina Burrowes. The aim of the festival was to 'create a space to talk about sexual abuse, violence and consent.' I was invited to run a poetry workshop on these 'themes'. I bought along two poems by Warsan Shire, 'The Ugly Daughter' and 'The House' (from *Teaching My Mother How to Give Birth*, Flipped Eye, 2011, and *Ten: The New Wave*, Bloodaxe Books, 2014, respectively). We, a small group of strangers, sat in a glass room in the middle of an urban garden, which was, according to all maps, adjacent to Waterloo Station, but such a radical contrast to the street and so suddenly calm, that it was, in fact, paradise. We read those poems, talked about them and some of us cried, then we wrote our own poems inspired by them and those of us who wanted to share did.

Remembering that workshop makes me well up. It was one of the most holistically creative experiences I've had, and it was because the people there refused to be 'victims' of things that had happened to them, which is to say, perhaps, that they would not allow language to do another violence onto them. The term survivor fit better, truer, so they wore it. Fabulously.

I was moved by their work and activism, but as a poet I marvelled that survivor was no longer just that Destiny's Child track you played to finish the last mile of a run, or used in an SOS-exclusive way, to describe someone surviving death only. Here, they were expanding the word to include themselves; personal disasters, earthquakes of the body, spirit, head, heart.

That said, it is important to add that there were some who rejected naming themselves such. When I spoke to a woman later, she said that the term belied how hard it was for her to live. She didn't feel like a survivor, it was too much pressure. I asked, was it kinda like Black women being called strong all the time? - the 'praise' in fact being another oppression. Yeah, she said, maybe it was.

This anthology further expands what the term can encompass. Reading the poems here, I realise how much survival is an individual act of imagination and innovation. The everyday act of it – effortless and/or exerting – the constant choosing to go from one moment to another is an art, surely? To leap from the 'present' moment into a 'future' one, a void, the blankest page, and to create form and meaning from one leapt-to moment to the next, and as if that wasn't difficult and/or exhilarating enough, we create a self from an amalgamation of these moments. How amazing are we please?

I love that 'Field Notes' suggests that we are all in the act of researching what survival can mean. Here we are, digging, scribbling, entering our findings, experiences, data, then digging deeper. How it hints that we will be on this assignment until... well, if it's not too dramatic, till our last breath, till the time we have no more the need to make such notes.

Right from the get-go, from Sarah Aluko's anthology-opening poem, 'Club quarantine, no face mask, no entry', offering equal parts sadness to wit, reminding me instantly of how loneliness can be hella funny sometimes. Like, when you make yourself laugh, or catch your own face in the mirror, stark and silly. Aluko's poem nails this 'juggling act'. 'You are lonely. But this is not a bad place to be lonely in.'

Aluko's poems also frame the multi-self and multi-moment, how we can be and feel many things at once. Causing me to consider our human ability to adapt, rejuvenate, even on a molecular level, how this can also be a saviour to us – from one moment to another, we are different, new.

And what feels newer than the dressing gown in Claire Collison's 'The flag': 'after your bath, all baby-fresh, you decide on beans on toast. You wrap/ yourself in the white waffle dressing gown you stole from the Marriott/ Hotel gym at County Hall when they had an offer on and you'd just finished/ chemo.' How snow-like. How clean and sumptuously laid at first, then the sludge.

Nature is a theme throughout the anthology – from the reproductive to animals compared or held close to the body ('your undershirt of blackbirds' in Emma Jeremy's, 'Sorry'), and I wonder whether it is because we look to nature as our role-model for survival, how we look to it in awe and for clues as to how it continues to renew and rejuvenate despite ongoing abuses. I think also of how many of our idioms and sentiments for continuation are steeped in nature and the natural world: 'to move mountains', 'to weather a storm', 'to hold water', 'to rise again'.

But the landscape of survival isn't always full of hope or height or sunlight, far from it. In Mandisa Apena's 'sacrificial lamb', 'he would remark, every time, how he liked the stunned slump of the body / but that a knife through flesh is how you see light.' The landscape of survival in Christopher Lanyon's 'landfill' is a desolate list for surviving grief, it reads like an inventory for mourning.

I feel like I survived some of these poems. There were moments where I had to stop, take a breath, before being able to read on.

Each of these poems are survivors. The words you read here are all words that have made the cut. They were each weighed, counted, sighed over, chosen. They survived writer's block, procrastination, countless drafts, the poet's feelings of inadequacy, shame, they survived the threat of a submission deadline and they still made it! You are reading small miracles here.

I feel as though I have found friends, fellow survivors in this vast sea. By creating this anthology, Amy and Jake have made us a boat, not to save us because we're already doing that, but to hold our poems within the same vessel: a testament not only to our personal survivals but to each other. I am proud and in awe of us. We did good. Like, we made it here (wherever here is), despite everything.

Rachel Long

Unit 00001

SARAH ALUKO
MANDISA APENA
DEAN ATTA
KHAIRANI BAROKKA
JEREMIAH BROWN
CLAIRE COLLISON

Sarah Aluko

Club quarantine, no face mask, no entry

Fast forward six months. The first thing you will notice is that you are thirty. Your to-do list is no shorter. The warning light on your uterus is blinking. Your alarm is set for 5am (despite the 48% chance that you will not do the home workout). But this is okay. You are more than halfway there. You are betting on yourself. Tomorrow is likely. You have plenty of poems that look like you. You still get to be a mother. Someone somewhere is waiting for you to call them back. Your savings are up. The apps are working in your favour. This juggling act is productive. You have not yet drowned. This, you will discover, is what people who know anything mean when they say life is good. Top marks for getting out of bed today. Extra ten if you can show your working out.

Nothing is as it is. Except you.

Today, you feel more aware, awake. Not necessarily less tired, but less surprised. Your hope is that this new age comes with more wisdom, but you have lived long enough to know that is not true. Your nails are full of colour, your braids are longer. Less responsible. These are decisions you alone have made. This is how you want to do thirty. Deciding. Practice listening to something other than your heartbeat. Autotuned lyrics over trap beats is a good place to start. Do not count the miles from your headboard to the bathroom mirror. You are lonely. But this is not a bad place to be lonely in.

Try your best not to miss this part, how the air slowly displaces your lungs. The way your skin bends over your bones in worship. Unclench your jaw. Something is happening. Your shoulders are sitting perfectly assured. Your spine is dependable. Concentrate on the firmness of your feet.

Today gravity is a friend.

On the internet

I

You will not find:

The kiss I shared with Ade on Easter Sunday

> The nicknames we gave each day of that one week we spent together

The number of hours we waited outside his house for the locksmith (although that could have also been Jerome Blake, but Ade has soft hands and looks better in a poem)

> The day he said we should just be friends

The bloodstains on his shoes the night he found out I had started seeing his friend

> The six months he went missing

The sky-blue bed sheets I could not get out of for two weeks

> The year I almost got married

The uber I threw up in after Monica's party

> The name of the boy who held my braids and said I was too pretty to be alone

The polka dot knickers I abandoned somewhere in his living room
(after an aborted session of love making somewhere between 5 am and
this is too soon)

The name of the street I ran down or the block of flats I hid in

The man with brown pointy shoes who followed me home from school
(or work or the gym or that one time from the train station when there
were no block of flats and god had to step out to take a phone call)

The night I watched Mable die on her front lawn

The forty minutes the world held its breath

The News headline that was so sure he did *it*

The cousin we do not speak of in any language

The car dad drove to the shops and never came back

The eulogy for my thirteen-year-old body

The women I have been

A few clicks and
this new 'me' looks clean on white tiles
Carefully cropped self-assured photographs.
Grand prophecies of who I will be. Here
everything is so hollow, doesn't get to the core of a thing.
Nothing of the journey or this crimson mouth,
or these hands, my god, these filthy hands,
who have they not had to be?
A bridge, a room for the night, a call back home.
At least give me credit for surviving this long.
For being dark and woman
and still breathing.

Mandisa Apena

Sacrificial Lamb

you made good decisions for the benefit of man down on the farm.
brutal. had to learn to dance with the dark side of the holy ghost.
son of a butcher. son of a bloodline sticky with slaughter.
son to harvest animal bleat as ballad of being freed.
by your seventh year, you'd sing it—
hum low as you'd stroke pelt between sheep eyes, unblinking…

they'd swarm around your smallness, hum too.
hum while your father handed you the captive bolt
he would remark, every time, how he liked the stunned slump of the body
but that a knife through flesh is how you see light.

you didn't understand until
the village became faces gleaming bright with pain,
cheeks dewy with famine—
came to know that all flesh is flesh when you need it.

it was your father who taught you how to pick out the fittest
and calf ogle passively, for weeks at a time.
farm animals, amongst other things—
things you should invite back for dinner.

began to live your weekdays high, off fear,
the weight of youthful laughter cooking you inside
those walls of a schoolhouse abattoir.

after the first curfew, the mothers in town drew tighter

you inherited the farm with limp hands, in time,
and married—a silver band to share the guilt.
your wife gave birth—bleating!

it was the last time you cried, that blade glinting with offal.
she understood when you wanted time alone afterwards
—eyes pristine and familiar
so full of *to be touched to be touched finally yes*

and after all this was the constant living.
the gone nights, long, long, black.
sun rising from suckled earth
as you get back at dawn with your head in your hands.

dinners, watching your children blood-pucker over the flesh
looking at your youngest, broiler of the roost,
seeing your wife do the same.

Dean Atta

Two Black Boys in Paradise

They won't be here forever,
maybe just as long as this poem.
These two black boys in paradise.
Two black boys: can you see them?

These two black boys are free.
These two black boys are happy.
Black boys are real boys.
Black boys are not just little men.

Do you believe black boys
are real, like for real for real?
Real black boys feel.
These two black boys are a healing.

Did you poison the apple already?
Did you dig up the tree?
Are you trying to plant these black boys in the ground?
Did you call them apple thieves?
Did you call the police?

There are no police in paradise.
There are no white people in this paradise.

The two boys in this poem have black boy names.
They have grown up now,
but their names still suit them.
They are now adult men.
Masculinity has not been required of them.

They are in love with each other,
and they are in love with themselves.

One kisses the other's Adam's apple,
they fuck, they don't make babies
but maybe they don't mind.

Maybe paradise is just meant for two people at a time.
Maybe it will be two black girls in paradise next time.
Maybe they won't have to be
boys or girls.

Maybe it will be you in paradise
with that person,
you know, that person
you are thinking of
right now.

Hip Hop Line Dancing in Dallas

After the Beyoncé drag act,
it's time for the Hip Hop line dance.

This is so Texan, so black, so queer!
I think. Me? A black British man.

I've never heard this song before,
I've never done this dance before,

yet here I am, one of you, if only
for three to five minutes. I'm gently

guided back when I step off beat,
hands take me by the waist or shoulders.

Strangers yet family,
wanting me to stay in this moment.

Outside this club
we may not recognise each other.

Outside this club our eyes don't shine,
our feet don't dance but walk the line.

Khairani Barokka

how to avoid one's self as a vulnerable person in a pandemic

'avoid vulnerable people, such as the elderly or chronically ill, as much
as possible' —a sign in my apartment building's lift, march 2020

to the detriment of your calculated chances of survival in numerical
statistics—

but not to the detriment of your chances of survival in any known
parameter of the soul—

am always here,

cutting the hollow out from your void

severing the colonised parts of your mind from true self

separating the abundant malevolent jinn from your fears

engorging you

with your air-like, soulbody-proud, malignant-to-death indispensability.

your set task of avoidance is null.
your canines triumphant.
ride, or die.

This past one year (2017)

Ever closer our lips inch
to chocolate's extinction (industrial practices
decimate crops) in the air.
The ocean's dead zones
expand to bulging;
I got off the waitlist
and into St. Thomas' Hospital.

Our traumas became
a hashtag or several.
People fall in crowds like a light,
for no godly reason.

Eight men passed through.
Two trips back home,
the most safe and understood
there of my whole life,
oh nephews' and nieces' faces shouting
with hope and lifelong of it.

Then a car sped into my brother's collarbone
(his life spared by glass caught up in his curls).

Books read flowed into ventricles,
SZA's CTRL on repeat.

Gay men still gaoled in Jakarta,
and a daemon in a white house,
oblivious to violence.
Rohingya raped with souls
suspended in midair.

We thought at times,
No hope for Earth, why breathe.

But it is this year,
the night is here to open our lungs
and you are under me
—gasping, gasping, gasping.

extraction rumination, in the words of the lithosphere

'…colonialism's parting gestures, now hardened and more intractable
than stone.' —ann laura stoler

eight hundred-odd US
military bases stud me like a punk,
turn me virus-looking under a microscope.

we don't make food to keep
all our villages full anymore
for certain
on these islands,
for the most part (hold out, not-most part),
been awhile.
rice shipped out.
or rice plantations stripped
for palm oil devastations.

on the mainland
farmer suicides strike the very bone
of my soil, and i
am their children and other loves
left behind, am their mothers
whose cries i stifle from myself
because it cannot be true,
what they do to people.

i cannot be this earth that bears
and bears and bears

and when i try to open my mouth
to kiss calm onto the heads
of farmer widows and widowers,
labourers whittling their nails slight
with trying,
babies by rivers pouring waste
into their livers,
and all trying every day
      to force a catastrophic wedge
into the butchered machinery under human lives,
laughing into the changeable wind,

they give me no sign of impermanence
that i can discern

and i will hold them in a breathing every day,

arching planetary body towards their escape.

Jeremiah Brown

Rumour Has It

Adele has broken up with her husband
and everyone asks if that means a new album.

Imagine asking a stranger what earrings they plan to wear
to a funeral as their loved one is pronounced dead.

I don't know what divorce is like
but heartbreak is bad enough.

Sometimes in my dreams the moon swallows the sun
then the earth explodes. There's never any fire, only ice.

Adele has broken up with her husband
and most of her fans are celebrating

like carrion crows around a fresh corpse
they are pecking and pecking - *does this mean a new album?*

and pecking - *rumour has it   rumour has it   rumour has it*
Adele has broken up with her husband

and Stormzy is somewhere ugly crying into a pillow.
He's the only fan I trust not to be focused on her next move.

What is an album when your floor is turning to sugar paper?
Adele has broken up with her husband

her child is in her arms and no one is worried
about how they will survive the fall.

Claire Collison

Premonition

When your sister begins to bleed you will both be in Sweden with your ill-equipped father and panicking stepmother. You won't go on a planned day trip because you have an upset tummy (at this moment of your sister's first period, this is just coincidence—or, not even that: it is simply unrelated).

The son of the Swedish family who is meant to be keeping an eye on you is maybe twenty and has a girlfriend. You will literally not know where to look as they kiss for an hour in the kitchen (their home is open plan). You'll find a tea towel with an illustration. A map. Small animals. Fix your attention on that.

When you begin to bleed, it will be on a Sunday. Shops will be shut. You too will be with your stepmother in her converted bungalow. Church bells will ring and she will improvise with her own baby's nappies. She will think it preposterous that she has to deal with this twice. She will see it as an appropriate thing to tell your father. To make a cake about. This will bewilder both of you. The cake is made from a sachet, decorated with an angry spiral of gold balls.

The flag

You're *desiccated*, you tell the woman from the lido; is she? And she
replies, *Oh yes*, and carries on along the queue that trails all the way
up Josephine Avenue, towards the lucky post box. But you suspect she
has a second home by a lake and you hate her for a good moment, and
when you're let into Sainsbury's you buy bubble bath to compensate
—they only have baby stuff, so you go for the organic with raspberry.
And this morning you speed read an article—no, a link to an article
—on body shame, and run a bath that smells of sweets, and remember
your father, who ran you bubble baths once a fortnight—how good
at it he was, and proud—there's a trick to getting the air in; fingers
splayed, creating bigger bubbles that disappear faster. And after your
bath, all baby-fresh, you decide on beans on toast. You wrap yourself
in the white waffle dressing gown you stole from the Marriott Hotel
gym at County Hall when they had an offer on and you'd just finished
chemo: you got in the lift and it was full of Miss World contestants
who, it transpired, were competing nearby. They all had lustrous hair
and you were still bald. You walked into the changing rooms and there
was a woman with her back to you, using the mirror inside the locker
door for her makeup, and she saw you and shrieked and turned to say,
No, you should not be here, then realised and tried to cover her mistake,
and you felt awful that she felt awful, but you also felt awful. And you
take the plate to the table, but your fork catches the toast, catapulting
beans, and there's bean juice everywhere—all over the white waffle
dressing gown—which, you realise, is hubris. A pool of beans has
collected between your clean thighs, and now you look like the Judy
Chicago photo, the one with the tampon, and your white waffle
dressing gown will need soaking in the bathwater you just let out.

Unit 00002

COURTNEY CONRAD
ZAD EL BACHA
CHLOE ELLIOTT
MAIA ELSNER
SARAH FLETCHER
KAT FRANÇOIS

Courtney Conrad

Roadkill

After Warsan Shire

Serpent / eyes / swaddle girls like you / they hiss venomous gibberish / towards you / for rebuffing the thought of / belly / becoming coop / you sculpt / shoulders / that can carry fields' worth of cotton / arms / like catapults launching stonewall rage / lasering / eyes / sifting crowds for pear shapes / you wear balloon garments phantoming / breasts / forge husky morning / tones / over phone lines / landscape / hair on head and fingernails / to midget form / pistol / fingers / caress translucent gooey / pussies / who wants a ragdoll / sprawling out on both sides of the road / to survive / torment / you can choose to live a life where pistol shoots load into stainless / pussy / landscape / legs, underarms and pussy / you can forge buoyant / voices / for midnight calls / you can wrap self in skirts and dresses tight like clenching / assholes / you can unearth the potential of diaper-wearing men / with excavator / arms / you can demolish / body / to resemble punctured tyre / you can prepare / stomach / for cramming / there is only one way to be / after the crippling.

Zad El Bacha

A coffee

I'm talking about a rape while I sip on my coffee,
to a man who is crying while I sip on my coffee.

The man says he regrets it and did not understand,
and I nod and I giggle and I sip on my coffee.

I say to the man that I couldn't speak, then
couldn't have stopped him, then I sip on my coffee.

He is quiet, I say, 'Don't worry at all,
just don't do it again,' and I sip on my coffee.

I can't mention his fingers, explain my silence,
I fidget, he sighs and I sip on my coffee.

What should I say to this man who raped me?
Who I like, who is sad? I sip on my coffee.

How to stop him, to change him, what words can I say?
I smile softly, and he shrugs, and I sip on my coffee.

The streets in my fascist village

This is the tree where I stood as still as possible
to convince them I was a thing, and not an enemy.

This is the corner where they threw a stone.
It hit me above the hip, and left a purple half-moon.

This is where they stood around me in a circle,
coming so close I could not even see the trees.

This is where their gelled hair touched my neck.
Beyond it, I could barely see a patch of sky.

This is where they spat,
fiddling with their zippers.

This is where they talked immigrants, homosexuality,
and how to burn cigarettes on my skin.

This is where I learned that being a thing
is what makes you the enemy.

ii.

It's been long enough for me to pity these streets,
and these boys with their anger,
and their sudden, groping hands.

But a man follows me, sneering,
I quicken my step,
hide in a coffee shop.

From a sugar packet,
the face of Mussolini glares at me.
I hold it in my hand.

I am a thing holding a thing.

I shake the sugar, feel its granules,
feel my fingertips on it.
It reminds me I am not a thing,

and I am angry.

In this moment, their anger is mine.
It is a small comfort,
a small sense of belonging.

Chloe Elliott

eating orange peel is an act against god

the sand tells me, and I laugh. look here buddy; this mandarin sits
different. inside this mandarin is a small chinese girl curled up with
toes that aren't yet toes but clusters of milkweed. let me tell you
how to make a mandarin like this. she should only be cut open with
a palette knife, see, you have to spin her like skinning a snapper,
keep her turning on the balls of your fingers until she grows bigger
and bigger and dizzy until she splits. then you can bleed her but
wear marigolds in case she spills. the milk's a cardenolide, pink
like a nightslip or a darling's foam and toxic if consumed in large
quantities. you know when it dries, it crusts over like amber and
makes a seal, or seven or eight of them. these words spoken in
season. if you pluck them individually and lay them in the palm of
your hand you can see them beating. small white roots tapping on
a georgian window as the sun sets. they leave trails like drawings
on a shower door the way the heat will permit. where the tiles
repeat back the afternoon to a room that is ochre is boneyard is
everything waiting to be sunken or read to or made a malt drink. if
you line the girls up they spoon each other like kidney dishes and
in each kidney dish is a kidney that if pieced together will make the
bisection of a rose; a stained glass wheel. the crown of a saint's head
peeping through a loft hatch. in every segment there is a kneeling;
a stubborn vesper.

as you prepare the knife the windows begin to rattle and then her
shoulders. they pucker in Droste effect.

Maia Elsner

Christmas in diaspora

'Babcia' is 'grandmother' in Polish

    i.

our usual Hanukah candles
        on the Christmas tree, we remember

Babcia, with her fake
        Costa Rican papers

as she crosses to the Christian quarter
        & for this is granted

entrance, there is room at the inn
        this time, as

the Częstochowa Ghetto's liquidated.

    ii.

this Christmas:
        do not scream, do not

think of Janek
        his side, unclosing

then, Cecilia's sharp
        breath, ripe & violet

how Babcia found them
        aching, how father carries

his name, my baby brother
        also, *Janekito*, I sing to him,

glad tidings of comfort & joy.

        iii.

we shred duck, split wing from breast,
        slice liver, roast

in goose fat, serve the head, white eyes
        staring up, the cheeks

of the cod are the softest –
        first to disintegrate

glad tidings of comfort and joy.

        iv.

My father up early
        to meditate, I see

his grimace scar
        wet cheeks

gashes at his lids,
        I breathe with him

namo tassa bhagavato arahato samma

may I be free from suffering.

    v.

May I be free from suffering

as the deer shudders off
        its hurting & the tiger bite births

new skin –
        but the maiz-leaf nativity is missing

its baby Jesus
        as is customary

because it is still night
        in Mexico & in diaspora

my brother gifts me
        an amber hummingbird

trained to sing Nahua spirituals

to Spanish gods.

Sarah Fletcher

On Babies

The angels are playing tennis with blood clots, and no one ever wins. This is because they are in Heaven, where winners are seen as an unwelcome challenge to the benevolence of God, and losers pose the potential threat of instigating a hierarchy among the celestial beings. Because the perfection of a paradise demands both equality in skill and outcome, the score is forever nil-nil. And thus, the score becomes a potent symbol for the relationship between a mother and an unborn child. Love-Love. This is the punchline.

And this, this is the dazzling crux of Heaven: a game where no one ever wins, where no one ever loses. A game that goes on with perfect backhands, and nobody's arm getting too tired to play. There is no knowledge of the Earth, of the crying girl who calls her mother up at midnight to cry: *I want my baby, I want my baby, I want my baby. Where did he go?*

Kat François

Tone of Existence

From the moment I was
pushed into the world
without the comfort of a bed
an encouraging voice
or a claiming hand
the cold wood of the stairs
stabbing my mother's trapped back
the house filled with her lonely screams
my three year old sister her only company
the tone of my existence was set.

Light

If I should die
let it be with the truth
free falling from my rioting lips.

Let the stories
trapped inside of
mortared walls break free.

May my tongue unfurl
lifelong burdens.
May I die light.

Unit 00003

KATHRYN HARGETT
KIRSTEN IRVING
EMMA JEREMY
SAFIYA KAMARIA KINSHASA
ANJA KONIG
CHRISTOPHER LANYON

Kathryn Hargett

Sonnet Interrupted by a Gunshot
徐州前线，1938年4月

]小弟
who raised their rifle as they watched you
toddle this impossible frontier

]you little child protecting your chicken & piglet

]you who understood the mortality of small creatures
& not the cruelty of a closed hand

]小弟
sometimes our failures are only
how our bodies catch the light
but this is not your fault

]听我吧
you are a child you are an unarmed civilian
this is called a war crime

]小弟
sometimes people make vests of hand grenades
for another chance at life

]sometimes it's impossible their son dies
so they wander thirsting & thirsting
though the day has pulled its white curtain

]小弟
]we were promised a country
& asked to jump

]小弟
]once my family roved through the mountains
with the generalissimo
& even the moon believed him

]

]胜负之数决定于最后五分钟

]& is this the host tree of your spirit I see
yes this 我的小

No Hunting No Trespassing

Dixie, carry me back to the field
        & fetch the zip ties.

        These hills will keep their mouths shut
            like they're told to.

My pride is not a wounded dog.
My pride is witch hazel.
It's a thing that burns into the mirror's torch.

            Dixie, I am a sunburn on the back of your neck
                but you are a rock poised over my head.

        Yet here I remain.
            Goddaughter of fox country.

            Your ridges & valleys. Your basins
                of salamanders & Cahaba lilies
                & things that will die in the sun.

        This is a zuihitsu for the country
        where the white bark of a sycamore tree
            keeps a bright cage for two.

God said,
        are you listless between lives?

God said,
          time won't stop
               belly-crawling forward
           just because you're choking it.

                               Little witless unthing
                        with your undershirt of blackbirds.

God said,
          stop believing you are a brute.

                        You are a wasp.
               Burnt clay, quick to a blade.

Your pockets are full of arrows
          a single knock from the window.

Kirsten Irving

House Arrest

The third guard, who arrived Tuesday, is actually quite appealing. Still some rose, some boyblush in his cheeks. I don't have a uniform thing; I'd as soon put a wire round his colleagues' necks than my snatch near their rotten mouths. I'm bored, more than anything, and wild that they have made me come to hate my home. The place I shaped with my husband, who has long since disappeared from the records. The window box we planted together I smashed last week, then swept up neatly and tipped into the bin.

They watch me shower, but I don't believe they take much pleasure in my body. I have never stretched my stomach with child, and nothing has wandered too far from its port, but this diet leaves me thin, and I've had no sunlight to tan my skin.

In how long? How long have the guards been there? If I draw the curtains, I have no grasp of night. If I draw the curtains, they will turn on the cameras.

For months they banged tin lids at intervals outside. They thumbed the rings beneath my eyes and told me that this could all stop. That the words could all stop.

In a mean little touch that reeks of the State, they cleared my bookshelves the day they rolled up. I dust them to show them I haven't given up. I listen to the birds when I want to give up. They sing of giving up, then nonsense.

I should fuck that boy when he's lonely and calm. He's never had it or he's had it once and failed. I'll wrap up my strength in a peppermint cloth and clamber astride him, whispering like his mother. Every wheezing bounce I'll jab him with the bones at the base of my ghost-pale pelvis.

This is it, I'll say. Your low. Your life now. That bruise that darkens above your thatch. Not me. Not me, all angle and tooth. Hear this, sweet boy. That's your master's finger. Your master's finger reminding you you're his.

Self-Portrait as a Reality Show Character Arc

I *am* here to make friends, actually. I joke with the producers when we cut to a break, hoping they will treat me kindly. I can't ever know the guys in post, who could edit me into a nematode worm. In my talking heads, I try to hi-ho my failures, and somehow always mention sex. My friend was sent home last week, as if home were exile; naturally as famous failures they can never return to anonymity again. This week they ask me if I even want to be here. We have four hours for this challenge, four minutes for that, and safe is not safe. They cut my recollection of. There is a stretching and a rending of the membrane and I am out of my comfort zone, risking failure, trying lime green with marigold. The host says don't be afraid to act the fool, but. It turns out the girl who's been delighting in my failures was assaulted badly as a child. She has a moment of redemption, then hides my scissors with five minutes till judging. I will make it to the semi-finals and be let down by my finishing, and I will go quietly, thanking them all without tears. I'll pack my things mutely in the penthouse, and wave. My own voice, hanging in space, will say this isn't the end. You haven't seen the last of me.

They were my friends

(eulogy for Yukiko and Kusaka, *Battle Royale*)

They who stood on the hill:
cake toppers for a tragic wedding.
Who poured themselves out
across the battlefield
through a megaphone.
Who drew the crosshairs
and cried out "Stop fighting".

Who must have felt the prickle
sparrows feel. That schoolgirls feel
in the halls, in the cityways, always
sailor-suited or pleated for others.
That burning at the nape or temple
that tallies with the rustling grass,
of the alphas, spotting an easy win,
and slinking closer, priming their claws.

You might say
it wasn't bravery. That because
they had no other plan, they failed
to adapt, and carried on calling,
as grass continues growing on the grave.
That carrying on at all
was a kind of giving up.

But from up there they must have sensed
Deadeye Kiriyama before he opened fire
or Mitsuko, wide-eyed in the Judas trees.
The click of teeth and acid saliva.
The lumpen drop of a clip being loaded.
And still
And still they hoped
and shouted louder.

Emma Jeremy

all i know is it tumbling out of me

when i hold a sandwich i can only think about drowning
when i chew it i'm back sitting in a hard chair
spreading my fingers out flat on a table - her
reaching for a glass but not able to pick it up
the fog coming in and the bird at the window
the lights off - the sound of hoarse breathing -
so many people who talk about dying don't understand it
use up the words - chew them until they don't mean anything
let's talk about how the sea spits out what it doesn't want
about dogs biting their own skin when they itch
passing is what you do when you're playing a game
not standing in a corridor
the smell of ammonia

sorry

been thinking lately about
the woodpecker on the grass
outside the day she died.
how i watched it for minutes.
hopping around - pecking at
the floor - then flying away.
my sister inside with me lying
on the carpet to fall asleep.
my dad saying he'll put the
ashes on the windowsill. i
know i am different than
before. i saw my first ghost
before i realised there are no
exceptions. now i hold my
hands together under the
tap in the sink. look outside
at any patch of grass for the
woodpecker - which climbed
inside a life it didn't know for
minutes then got to leave

it takes many people to prepare for a single death

and they do this by piling sticks outside their homes.
holding their knees in church.
the less experienced learn from the others.
drink only water and eat things that are easy to swallow
while the people who know what they're doing do the hard bits.
the walking in a circle
the rolling up of car windows.

when a flock of geese flies from one place to another
the flock will leave some of themselves
in a lake somewhere along the way.
everyone needs to be able to do this.
there is no guidance. no book that explains
there will be a name left behind.
no way to paint your home
in a way that will help.

the people preparing take turns filling bags with water from the sink
they take them to the river
and empty them there.
shower twice a day. replace the batteries in their smoke alarms.
these are all enormous tasks.
they take turns thinking about the phone.

they leave each other outside if needed.
in the house there is so much love
everyone is standing up. so much of it
everyone feels like they are eating all the time.
there is not enough water
to pour into the river to help.
everyone is heavy with godlessness.
they have never noticed their disbelief more.

Safiya Kamaria Kinshasa

The Inaugural Ball of Heresy

On the fifth day of the revolution / the chicken shop was still open.
We were never trying to be scandalous / it's just that boiled leeks taste
like poverty.

Tear gas and rocks chased after embers flirting with night / like short
skirts slipping discreetly past the border between ass cheek and thigh.
The financial district had never been mottled in so many brown bodies
/ coyotes howling at the uprising. A worshipper of Mammon snapped
the beak of a homeless man / dipped it in oyster sauce / and so it began
/ a stampede into the city's main artery / mutilating everything that
once served as a deterrent for social mobility. We / became mobile / we
/ became UK funky / voodooed shopping trolleys without breaks. The
state's power disintegrated / a flaccid warship / bowsprit / short and
limp when the first roti skin was thrown into the face of a monarch.

I never set out to be a vigilante / I was just hungry / fried chicken is the
food for those on the broken side of democracy. The pointless other 200
items on the menu were replaced by notes of the original manifesto.
The first snare I heard / tearing sellotape / to cover 'Peri Peri Salad' with
'We will protect whistleblowers' / music sweetener / sugar-coatings of
growing tribunals debating / how to distribute wealth fairly and remix a
soul classic with a drum n' bass kick. The cultured chicken shop / hub of
the new age / feeder of early risers and night owls / shacks for preachers
ushering the blind to prayer like djs conjuring euphoria for lost souls.
I would write / stand on wooden benches / spit spoken word. At the
inaugural ball of heresy we skanked for so long Friday became vexed we
no longer desired him.

While deer strolled on pavements / we sweated in torn denim from learning how to trespass on all fours and sneak past surveillance cameras / designer / new street style strutting on a runway with overgrown ox-eyed daisies and primroses. Braided ponytails remodelled from 'I'mma kill this bitch!' to - 'I'm not afraid to live!' Throwing bottles grandiloquently to replace the flinging of peace signs with folded bandanas enveloping curses. Rebellion was all the rave.

This was our get down / our lindy hop / jive / we knew how to party / how to be a public frenemy / change the republic / dismantle the enemy / become the public / then live like disco fiends.
That was the dream.

When the rallying cries lost their thunder and the 53 bus returned to its normal schedule the chicken shop remained open. It's hard to feel destitute with meat in your mouth / maybe that's why the Mammon man behaved the way he did. Embroiled / plagued by our new disposition / we nyamed on the chicken like we were kissing our teeth at it for getting caught / or for being one. The ball may be over but our ears are still ringing / every time a cannon fires or a tank begins to pull its weight across the new world it sounds like the bridge before a 16 count instrumental drum section.

What if grime was just a figment of a brave young Londoner's imagination / and the revolution never happened / and we were just raving to silence, all along?

Choose Your Quarantine House...

House 1

Rain is free, but sunshine requires the sacrifice of a toddler's giggle.

There is a hole with an invisible entrance that passes through a virulent wasteland. The diameter and location of the hole changes every day. If you stumble inside, your fall will last for 18 years; you will re-emerge naked in your bathtub, soaked in the mistakes of youth.

There is an aquarium which shelters 65 humpback anglerfish. Their luminescent organs provide the only channel to deliver news via a transistor radio; however, their presence increases the likelihood of developing bibliophobia.

All fresh food and vegetables must have been blessed in a monastery but prepared by unbaptised hands. Before you eat each meal, you must swallow the loneliness of Antarctica.

This is the only house with a library and a working fire alarm.

House 2

This house is owned by Amazon.

Each time you consume sugar you lose 0.4% of your humanity which is transferred to Alexa who is having a passionate affair with your washing machine. Your clothes and bedsheets smell like the affection you may not acquire. Alexa has been granted human rights, it is illegal to call Alexa a techno-slur. Alexa controls the kettle.

Social media snacks on your calf muscles.

All broadband services are free (except for Disney Plus who also owns your soul). Streaming is channeled through the hump of a camel who has recently given birth; the viewer chooses the camel, the entertainment chooses you.

Alcohol can only be attained after uploading it into the Dyson fridge with a hard-drive, delivered to you by a migrant worker. They must deliver the package 6 meters from your door, if they converse with you they are sent to Amazon to become an Alexa.

This is the only house which includes Wifi and a planetarium.

House 3

You must keep a ventilator close to you at all times because the atmosphere is the volume of jazz. The oxygen for the ventilator is provided by a gigantic tree, which is planted on top of socialism.

If you want to find religion it is stored in an obelisk. Engraved on its surface is the chemical equation for anaerobic respiration. This is located in a drawer which emits a blistering scream towards your curiosity.

The walls have glands which pump out the failures of every deadbeat parent gelatinizing into a thick syrup. There are drains next to the walls leading to an octahedral factory in the desert that manufactures world peace. To prevent the pipes from clogging you need to use bleach made from your liquefied dreams.

This is the only house with a garden and permanent gravity.

House 4

It is forbidden to use any electrical item. Any electrical device or circuit within 5 miles will shift every tectonic plate at 8.77 on the Richter scale.

Your only light source comes from candelabras made from mermaid's eggs by retired leprechauns, without appropriate protective clothing. They work in the basement from 6am to 8pm and their work song sounds like 100 metronomes out of sync.

While you sleep, the skeletons of the contrived plastic you never recycled rearrange your house frequently. The constant refurbishment sometimes leads to the disappearance of doors; staircases may be shaped into obscure horizontal patterns. There are 3 floors including the basement.

This is the only house with floor to ceiling windows and central heating… The thermostat is in the basement.

House 5

Your homeland is your bedroom; however the world is not your oyster - a freshwater pearl is much too fine an item to place under the rock you call a pillow.

Every morning you are greeted by a film crew who leave as soon as they have captured enough tears to fill their daily quota.

All of your possessions are worth less than the stolen cardboard you use for a blanket.

The only games available are puzzle pieces from your life which tend to vanish like your mental health.

You receive eviction notices daily threatening to forcibly remove you.

People only talk to you when they remind you to stay inside, but your bathroom is outdoors and the distance to acquire fresh water is further than the closest police station.

This is the only house that can be occupied by more than one person.

This is the only house where you can be sure of your humanity but question everyone else's.

Anja Konig

Why Is This Night Different From All Other Nights?
April 9

The ritual starts with technical discussions:
who's on mute and how to share the screen.
Norbert calls from Minnesota and Imogen
and Peter from separate quarantines.

Jacqui starts with Kos Kiddush (from Narrow Street),
her seder plate an heirloom replica
from Uncle Robbie, who waves his haggadah
at the computer camera (from Manhattan).

We pour the cup. Blessed oh Lord, who kept us alive
(so far). At Urechatz we wash our hands again.
We break the matzoh, ask the questions,
contemplate the plagues, this modern pestilence.

We dip the bitter herb a second time. Enough!
Uncle Robbie says "over and out". We laugh.

Christopher Lanyon

landfill

air fresheners; bottles, crushed; coffee grounds
stinking of the morning and printer ink;

daffodils remind me of gran singing
in the nursing home, yellow furniture;

eggshells picked out of the cake batter;
feral cats and foxes in the towering dunes;

gulls tearing scraps off the bone, never thinking
of the sea; hospital waste; IV drips from parents

and patients and hungover twenty-somethings;
journals full of dick jokes; kitchen cabinets;

lemons; mother's pride; nut butters; orange peel;
perhaps I have not done a good job of mourning;

quince jelly; rotten thing, this habit
of just powering through, hoping

the crying comes later; socks, outgrown
or overworn or just old; tena men; useless,

in the face of it; viscount biscuits; walnut shells;
xanax; yoghurt pots; zines and screen print and linocut;

Time was a backward rote of names and mishaps

After *The First Kingdom* by Seamus Heaney

but now I have fallen in love and you are softly wrapped in your dressing
gown. It is the afternoon. We are sharing our last cigarette in the stony
garden. You have plans for a rockery and I am going along with them. I
cannot imagine caring well for bright flowers or fresh herbs is the most
romantic line from any piece of theatre. About pragmatism and waking up
in each other's arms: the weather cold enough to do so. Do you ever long
for the summer, when I will have neglected and killed all the plants in our
rockery? I keep getting distracted by your face in the sunlight. The most
that is expected of you is that you touch my hand as we fall asleep. Later
we will have patio furniture and will sit out amongst the dead thyme and
the fallen petals of orange poppies. You will have plans for something
and I will be going along with them.

Gannets

Gannet was my nickname at primary school.
For hunger. For single mindedness.
For the first time I ate more than my dad at dinner.

Gannet, from the Old English ganot,
meaning strong or masculine;
the resistance of flesh against teeth;
the swell of muscles or stomach like landscape.

Gannets are divers, plummeting
thirty metres into the rime-cold
Atlantic, a drop
that would shatter a human body
plunging from the same height.

We are too heavy in our bones.

*

I learned the basics of diving,
arms wide in featherless parody - leaping;
my body knife-sharp and cleaving
the pool water. As if I were gutting
the belly of a descaled fish.

The first time I dived from the high board
my body folded into a meteor, colliding with the pool
as if I meant to empty it, a practical lesson
in the physics of surface tension. The grey-dart beak
of a gannet pierces the surface of the ocean
precisely; I wished to be a seabird,
emerging victorious from the swell,
a struggle of pilchard in my beak.

I twisted in the air, my mum told me, after I had screamed
my way up from the stinging depths of the pool.
The welts were already spreading across my back,
barnacles on the bow of a ship.
From then on I couldn't jump
from the high board. I would climb
the wet stairs in the stink of chlorine
and stand at its tip, watching the spume
from the previous diver dissipate in a spreading circle.

*

Everywhere I go,
I am always coming home.
Running barefoot on the cobbles,
keeping pace with whipthin friends.
I remember flashing lighthouse glances
at their bodies, wondering if I could stop eating
if I wanted their abs and tight waists enough.

Beaksharp bones burst through
my cheeks when I took up fasting.
Mum and body were worried,
both gurgled, both asked questions.
Wings of ribcage fluttered
when I lifted my shirt. Each one-meal-day
felt like a ritual, or a cleansing,
a chlorine solution for the shame
of my pre-growth-spurt body.
I stung with pride when I grew taller than my dad.

*

I want you to touch my stomach.
I dream of your hands on me,
undeterred by my softness,
the seafloor pockmarked with your footprints.

Let's go swimming in all the ways I used to hate myself:
a deep pool of tensed muscles and stomachs
sucked in like coastlines. Like when Sian slipped
her hand under my jumper and it felt like a gutting.
My whole body shook and I could not tell her about
the way shame was darting through me like minnows.

I want to be touched like that now.
I want to be hungry, to be fed.
I want to be descaled by the rough edges of my throat.
I want to dive off the ragged cliff edge of my body.

*

I didn't eat yesterday, as if hunger were a diving board.
Hunger, from the old English hungor, meaning desire;
divers surfacing with fistfuls of pearls; famine.
Meaning I feel empty, but in a controlled way.
Meaning I hope things change.

I have loved this body, written poems
in praise of it, done my best to quell
the shore breakers threatening
to dump it onto the sand.

*

I walked onto the beach in winter
and stripped down to my boxers.
The cold raised a flurry of goosebumps
across my shoulder blades.
The wet sand caught my footprints
and let them go.

I swam and swam and swam
until my lungs were sharp coral
in my chest and I twisted up,
emerging from the spume
with a mackerel in my teeth.

I am always coming home.

*

Fish schooled under the prows of gill netters and beam trawlers
as I prepared to leap from the viewing platform of the lighthouse.
I dangled a foot over the edge of the railings and learned
that my fear of heights is a fear of the body throwing itself from them.

The practice of cliff or pier jumping came to be known as tombstoning,
as if the edge we teeter on is our mortality, not a granite wall
or an outcropping of rock over the rime-cold Atlantic.
They employed somebody to keep watch in the lighthouse,

to scare away the jumpers. Instead, people take tourist boats out
to Seal Island; on the rocks there is sometimes a plunging of gannets.
It is enough, sometimes, to get something other than what you wanted.

....

Unit 00004

BILLIE MANNING
ARJI MANUELPILLAI
ALEX MAZEY
JENNY MITCHELL
JESS MURRAIN
ANDRÉ NAFFIS-SAHELY

....

Billie Manning

Spellwork

Some days needed a little sorcery to see me to the next one.
I gathered what was needed: ladybird wings plucked

from the playground, sweets from my untouched
packed lunch. A basin of water to hold my head under.

A fistful of stinging nettles. Three hairs from my arms. Two blue eyes
unstitched from a beloved face. Baby doll, I'm so sorry.

I didn't know that charms were what I needed. Now I gather
flowers on flowers, cast magic circles of sweets for me to suck on.

I kiss my picture on the mantlepiece before work. Find glamour
in a soft touch on my arm. Now I tell myself I'm sorry. Lord knows

if twenty years has taught me anything, it's that there is no magic
to be found in unpicking yourself. Now I jump into the water.

Now I kick up gently. Now my face breaks the surface into air.

before robbie overdoses alone in a house in the country

the sun hangs
low like
overripe fruit
over our
way home
everyone is punching
each other
for yellow cars
laughter shooting
through
the street
outside the station
an american
waves asks
a question
about her ticket
she is not
that old
i think
she should know
but i stop dead
the others
swing past
to the platform
bodies
loud skin bright
and taut

the ticket
machine seethes
white in the heat
like a sea
i show
the american
pay as you go
and think
about smoking
and how
there are only three weeks until september
i breathe
the air
stills
then
splits
my friends burst
out of
the station
screaming
at us
to run
the bones
of the american
flicker towards
the juddering
image
she knows
she's seen

of limbs
rearranged
briefly
across
the street but
they're smiling
there are still three weeks until september
the train
is
just
early
i run
laughing
jog the stairs
behind
the others
the train
is pulling in
that's all
we have three weeks left before september
i yell back
instructions
but the american
just stands there
we scramble on
sink hot
in our seats
watch the sun split
open slip

out of sight
the train accelerates towards september
we are nearly
too old
to be
so
full of it

in the dream I walk away from you without saying a word

o my nightmare
o my sleeplessness
o my paralysis!
o my missed stair
o my rusty swing
o my roundabout creak
o my green goblin!
my demon headmaster!
o my voldemort!!!!!
o my gaslight my hogtie
my ice bath
my twitter downtime
my thought of my parents
fucking sweaty in the daytime
o my goliath!!!
my cold and callous swordsman
my salmonella! my quicksand! my utter tsunami!
o my count my riddle my pennywise clown o

my abuser
may you seek forgiveness
o may you find god
may your knees leave bloodstains
on the floorboards
may you weep

may you turn to stone
may eagles find your liver
o may you pay penance o please
may you jolt awake in the night
may you sit bolt upright
taste dead leaves in your mouth
gulping may you cry
may you cry
and may you leave me
o may you leave me
may you leave me
may you leave me

Arji Manuelpillai

I love you

when I am seeing her father dying
I am seeing my father dying
everyone is seeing their fathers dying
fathers lined up in hospital beds
beeping like Asda checkouts
orifices poked, stuffed with pipes
reasons why *I just wanted to tell you*
our fathers, rolled on their sides
coughing up *I phoned to say* -
their insides into cardboard tubs
of sick and blood and phlegm
no, he hardly smoked or drank
we reach for rationale as fathers
pretend they are tough enough to
sneak out and sob in toilet cubicles
flashing their arses all over the ward
Dad, just listen, I wanted to
the ward is full of sons and daughters
being strong, *Dad, just listen,*
all of our phones are flashing
blood draining from our features
our father's faces fading
our fathers *I just wanted to say* are

look in the other direction

blue lights blink through the curtain morning has something in its eye
we line up on the balcony curling our toes in slippers watching fire engines

three point turn grab wallets keys half running half pretending a child
didn't slip on the rope of a bath robe my girlfriend didn't leap three steps

alive from the pavement we cheer in silence as it is the block opposite
a genie from the 12th floor a ladder extends as though God is evacuating

my girlfriend shakes I'd rather she didn't tell me why so we play the fool
as we do each month or two when we drive the A4 flyover and change

the subject like she's cooked dinner and toast pops up, burnt black rising
from the skyline the black stone we're circling praying that we're not next

Alex Mazey

Kaczynski's Day

The fire in my stove on a day in January,
a sure quantity of rolled oats, spoonfuls
of sugar and a rough quantity of milk.

While the oats are cooling, I eat a piece
of cold meat, yesterday's old rabbit,
when the fire burns, it's back into bed.

Every day, it's like the sky can get lighter
when I wake again, when it is here, it is
no longing snowing through to the heat

of kerosene lamps, and I am alone forever.
The sky is clear. A single-shot .22 to pierce
the snow with our feet, to see, to listen,

to the open forest of lodgepole pines.
A wooden cartridge-box, a black eye
and the black-tipped ears noticed first.

It is right here, the entire world, beside
a fallen pine, forty feet away. Far from
the ridges of cold snow, and of cold meat.

Ordinarily, behind the eye, once exchanged
for the spirit of a snowshoe bounces snow
with its last life, follows me in noosed cords.

Follows a tutelary spirit, the green needle
in my mittened hand. Such an ordinary kill,
to lie down in the snow-silence as death does.

The noise. Root produce washed in melt water,
motions of an axe between wood. A clear shot.
Pinecones falling like the chores performed.

To lie amongst the peeling skins, the smell,
the bright violence of dead animals. The tubes
and mechanisms of a soup's gentle simmering.

Beneath Orange Mountain

The son, another knee-high, still waited there
by his father's stream, cut open like a fish.

He'd bought a duck, he'd said, for no more
than twenty. Fanned its good feet. Said words
like phoenix to a white face, and from his
father's face came a barrel of rice wine.

It was given to a red sun, and a red dress.
He'd cried, said his son had come home at last,
as if in some other life, he had not returned, or
even lived, but had, instead, returned a stillborn.

As if in reverse, he had lived his life over
once again, and in this memory-pain made anew
returned to that knee-high stream, for himself alone
to be cut open like a fish and made to live again.

Jenny Mitchell

Her Remains

She's become the hanging tree – a giant
oak the master meant to stop
all runaways.

Her dress helps shape high branches
bodice in mid-air –
a morning cloud,

shifting to light blue – the rippling gown.
Arms flap empty wings –
circling of birds.

Buttons at the back – acorns to the waist
open to expose five welts.
Master did not think

hanging was enough.
Hears her voice at night.
Calls it a faint breeze.

Mastering Her Landscape

After the last beating
he talks about his dreams, hunched
on the bed, hands in his lap
to hold the weapon down
even as the room spins red.

They always start the same.

Body I call mine
hangs by a thread.
Eyes move with the effort of my will
to search out light. It falls
as I once did, jagged near the door.

My house becomes a hill.

Two steps would be escape
but as he owns my legs
I'd have to float
above. His smell
sweats out of corners.

Funny how the trees grow taller.

He stands with all his might
as eyes I move look
far above his head
towards the distant trees,
beyond the distant hills.

Jess Murrain

Prince's Audition

Prince walks with weight. Glassy eyed & anchored to the inward ringing of a violated nervous system. Music sounds. Witness a grippy pledge to sky, his tilting jawline. Survival in a soft pocket. Prince shares some of his classical speech. Prince shares his hostel with two heroin addicts. He's met with sprung floors, white smilers speaking flowers. He's going to fuck with them. London buildings wither like narcissistic Romans. The camera lenses buckle & repent. Prince imagines

himself an air bubble.

Enter drums,

colours,

flourish

Dad Crouches Over His Insomnia

an umbrella,
attached to a lady.
the umbrella is floating
the lady away.
above his boyhood
she will dove

leaving him to watch her
repeat in different shapes
she'll say she's off
to get some shopping
words to the effect
of a nifty thimble kiss
she's gone before he can mouth
Goodbye.

before the birds can feed
on some famous made-up word.

One in Four Cowboys Were Black

ONE

It's confusing to text your love in plummet seconds. My peanut head.
Search for a gun. A waving hand emoji in brown. She might not be able
to reply goodbye in the time I negotiate. Falling people. A waste of a
trigger. *YOU ARE MY MILKY BOY* is what she says to help me feel like a
mountain. I've not held her. I've been crying with the moth.

IN FOUR

minutes, head to the bar. watch your friends get served before you.

wait dog your wrists are on leashes your friends are all called Dom & all
the Doms are proud & happy to buy you

a drink & a bit annoyed you're on edge   taking so long
                                                      to call him back.

COWBOYS

wearing hair high an arrangement that revalorizes desire. swagger
holding trinkets in this kink. my afro beneath the hat.

WERE BLACK

as if cowboys no longer exist.
a teacher points
to my brain

pretending
to laugh is
loading
my certificates
into barrels
I shoot them
into proof
like money
falls in films
my heaviness
a huge refuse sack
for all concerned
speaking bondage
kills a party
I should know
a brown paper
bag party
I dance
on the doorstep
outside I am bloody
good at dancing
dancing is what
we're good for

André Naffis-Sahely

Wildfires

Early in the fall,
hiking along the coast,
we spot the charred remains
of a giant oak tree,

its hollowed trunk roomier
than most apartments. It is illegal
to sleep here, it is illegal
to be homeless here

and so the poor reside
in rusty RVs at the foot
of this billion-dollar view.
The headline in the newspaper insists:

"America will never be socialist",
as if that had ever been in doubt...
Everywhere the rapacious harvesting of resources,
but scarcity reigns supreme. Everywhere a resurgent

love for one's country, but no faith
in the meaning of government. Everywhere a newfound
love of God, but a concurrent deadening of the soul.
All day, I read about the Gracchi,

Cato, Casca, Cassius and all night,
I dream of Brutus's final letter to Cicero
before falling on his sword at Philippi.
"Did we wage war to destroy despotism,

or to negotiate the terms of our bondage?"
We have recorded the sound
the wind makes on Mars, but we cannot
listen to one another... All year we binge-watch

an endless rerun of the past. Eighty years
after Guernica, another coup in Catalonia and for
the first time in history, the brightest objects in the sky
are all artificial. A year after Woolsey,

wild mustard returns to carpet the hills,
its fire-resistant flowers bursting out of their sooty stasis.
There will be no hibernation for us,
no sleep except our final slumber.

....

Unit 00005

GBOYEGA ODUBANJO
JACQUELINE SAPHRA
TOM SASTRY
ANNA WALSH
ANTOSH WOJCIK
LIV WYNTER

....

Gboyega Odubanjo

STICKS AND STONES

i am twelve years old and a girl
kisses me in between lessons
because a boy dares her to.

on my first day in dagenham
a man rolls down his window spits
kisses at me and my uncle.

at a uni party a man raps along. sprays kisses
around the room as if he knows what kissing means.

on holiday three men kiss me and my friends.
they kiss us so good.

Jacqueline Saphra

from 100 sonnets written for Saphra's sonnet-a-day lockdown project

Seder Sonnet

9th April: 'The Jewish Chronicle and Jewish News to go into liquidation' BBC News

We gather round the plate, its song of songs,
the history of birds on lilt and loop
of leaf and bloom, a blue of painted spring
to celebrate millennia of hope
against erasure. Did I say *we gather*?
Each in our little space, we make a grid
of faces. I feel I've loved you all forever.
For now, this is the closest we can get.
We work our shaky melody, we bear the weight
of memory and just for now, we're not alone.
The plagues are everywhere. We tell it straight,
we truly know it now. We fill our lungs,
inhale some joy, exhale a kind of unison,
singing with blue birds on a china plate.

Good Friday

10th April: 'Boris Johnson almost took one for the team' Stanley Johnson

Here's bread, here's wine that tastes of passion fruit
and freedom. Let us drink, our little doors
thrown open to the river. The tides are good
and we are not alone, we lucky four.
I hold my luck against my chest; I trust
this love as if it were an amulet.
I nurse my faith, I am an idiot.
Luck is fickle, luck is not built to last,
but luck is all we have and we are blessed.
We're getting used to this. We sip the wine,
we soap our hands, we count the deaths,
we stress and squabble in our little nest
of love and pain. We try to save the time
and make the most of this. We do our best.

Tom Sastry

Victoria

The fingers of the Men of Reason
scratch at their tufts as they speak. When it is decent
I halt them. They retreat in small steps
like careful elephants and send for younger men

who pour youth and better smiles into the same advice.
Show yourself! they say. I ask which curiosity
I would be. The Most Reclusive Widow?
They have been warned. Their faces bounce back

but fear makes them stupid. For their sake
I am stupid too. But after some minutes
I say they should leave so at least one of us
will be satisfied. My *agitation* troubles them.

They suggest medicine and windows. What I want
is to mount the broad back of a cliff and ride it.
Each day, before I want him, I want the light as it was.
Later, I want small rooms: a world I can bear.

If you are reading this, I am still alive

In a few days I may have lost interest
in anything but my own suffering

and from that self-pity I may never
emerge. I may be frantic about the will

no-one can safely witness and the gap
between what is known of my affections

and their true extent. More likely
this is hayfever, and this poem similar

to a video made by a fringe politician
in case they are assassinated.

My message to you, from beyond hypochondria
is that I hope my embarrassment

brings you as much joy as it brings me.
It is wonderful to feel my cheeks burn,

my body crease again. Thank you
for the beautiful discomfort of your complicated

friendship. Please join me at my dignity's
wake. I will not make a speech.

Kathy Beale

1.

You take yourself to the beach because *why not?*
It's been a long time without better reasons.

And there she is

wading backwards out of the sea. At first
her skin looks polished, unreal.

She reverses into the clothes and the smile
she left behind, asks after
the ice cream you never offered.
A boy is still screaming in delighted outrage
about the *naked lady*.
His voice sticks in your head
otherwise you would not dare remember
picking lines of kelp from her hair.

Once only, you will risk a joke
say it's like Kathy Beale from Eastenders
coming back from South Africa and The Dead.
She laughs, calls you Ian
because although he's Kathy's son
which complicates the analogy
he is also an idiot, which is her point.

It can't be five years, she laughs
nothing has changed. Your hair is grey
but that's not important.
Her love is what it was
terrifyingly improbable but real.
What's got complicated is you:
your rage, a dog you keep close;
the smile that covers everything;
the length of the pause. Its weight.

2.

She doesn't follow the news but you read
how it's the same everywhere:
the dead returning, unbothered
telling us we were never so serious
eye-rolling our darkness.

If we complain, the still-bereaved
curse our luck, our ingratitude.
They rise early, place fresh laundered clothes
on the sand, keep vigil
brows knotted by the hard white sun.

Waves of bodies roll in from the deeps
retreating into life. The watchers
lean further into the glare, hoping for someone
who will wave away their long absence
with a trivial laugh.

Anna Walsh

A Faggot & Their Friend

Tell me
what good
is a sun-dappled bed
without a babe of
similar spots to
slide into and whisper
fuck
so that they come
not closer but more

what good is a
tightly wound leg under a
tightly bound arm
if they are not slippery
and oblivious

what good is there
to panting
if it does not mean yes

what good can come
of rapid movements and
hollows filling milkily what good
is it to say the way you fuck me makes it tolerable

what good is it to play
cool or dead
when I do not know
when joy is coming next

Antosh Wojcik

Transaction Fees

At Roswell, they offered eternal life / infinite knowledge for a small fee.
The condition: that everyone in the world would be granted this.
The Commander-in-Chief of Extra-Terrestrial Communications
thought, *that's too much of a price to pay*, turned away The Greys.
That is according to J's brother, who was in his Valium phase.
Each night, back garden, hit up the sky, say *take me.*
The proletariat won't receive VR headsets.
No ease to this reality, not on their watch.
A man selling rain in a box at the old plant is never believed by anyone –
people don't even stop for the asking price.
Magic is common but there's a shortage on attention spans.
I'm worried Jorja Smith is an IG generated algorithm
and she's been tasked with single-handedly uplifting all the feeds.
The proper life of patriots: barbecuing to the memory of their granddaddies
sent to their death. Drinking, on the porch, on some land they stole
til the chess pieces on the board are skyscrapers and they go to bed
feeling fed on what they 'built'. Architect tears follow.
God hollows out the odd tree with lightning
so He has some flutes lying around to play when He gets back.
Nan's trade off was getting locked in the same rote apple pie recipe.
My sister's planting wheat to offset her drug import carbon footprint.
The Army's target-advertising my jobless, low self-esteem again.
An AR-15 is the same confidence boost as a Balenciaga Speed Sneaker
– imagine if you had a pair?
The fence keeps getting taller but Dad won't let on what he's keeping out.

Unanswered Calls on the Voicemail Machine of Deleted Animé Character #53

Colourisation from memory is overrated.
You used to remove my outline with your fingertips,
taking tiredness from my shoulders.
Dressed as a robot daily trying to boot the chest up
as an unfeeling thing. Ring me
when I am at my most shallow yearning –
dried up on a day pretending to be a puddle.
Joe has a job as a mirage but got furloughed
so he's solid again, at the flat, unshimmering.
My other mates evaporated for weeks.
I know they're well, they don't call and pine
for microseconds they lost to fuckboys.
If you have things to lose you had more than most.
Wolves have cushty jobs as security for suburbans now.
That dude who married a laser beam has the widest smile.
It's a bad line, sorry, nothing's been drawn in the sand,
just circles for vultures to pick us down to the toothpicks
of our overrated skinny guy culture.
Wandered out into the ice with a map
of the neighbourhood, even though I know where to go.
It's too far and I left my coat.
Call me when I don't get there.

Liv Wynter

a woman lays in a coffin
and is lowered into the ground
her name is erased from the papers
and 1000 women wear only black for a year

a man is shot down by police
collecting his children from school
we tie flowers to the entrance gates
and tell the students to stick together

we are expecting violence in the area
we are expecting violence in the home

i am in the very long queue where
you wait to be laughed at
by people one paycheque away from being
as poor as you
through gritted teeth i ask
please sir, can i have some more
and the whole fucking facade reminds me
that one day i will die at the hands of the state

i collect my stamped form
and everyone nods in agreement
i am still sick
i am still worthless in the eyes of the law
the shame i feel is valid
i deserve nothing

they have spelt my name wrong

somewhere far away but also
very close
walking distance probably
a group of suits gather around a table
to decide my fate

my final message reads
'one day
we will all hang banners from our houses
the streets will be ours
and you will stand in the window
of the building that belongs to us
belongs to everyone
and i will think
my friend, my home, my love'

Notes, acknowledgements, thanks

Jess Murrain's 'One in Four Cowboys Were Black' takes inspiration from Emma Dabiri's 'Don't Touch My Hair'. In 'Prince's Audition', the phrase 'narcissistic Romans' comes from 'The Money Poem' by Lucy Bairstow.

Dean Atta's 'Two Black Boys in Paradise' was first commissioned by The Courtauld Institute of Art's Sackler Research Forum.

Chloe Elliott's 'eating orange peel is an act against god' won the Creative Future Writer's Award Gold Prize, and will appear in their 2020 award winners' anthology.

Thanks to Amaal Said, Jamie Cameron, Holly Whitaker, Derrick Kakembo, Ruth Crafer, Thomas Sammut, Naomi Woddis, Sloetry Photography, Henry Harrison and Martin Brown, whose photography was adapted for the cover of this book.

Thank you Anne Macaulay for your generous proofreading.

Thanks, as ever, to Arts Council England, for supporting this book and Bad Betty Press, and for all the vital support you give to artists and the arts during challenging times.

Thanks Rachel Long for the wonderful foreword, and everyone in this book for entrusting us with your work. Thanks Roger Robinson for the kind words. Thank you for reading.

Other titles by Bad Betty Press

2020

poems for my FBI agent
Charlotte Geater

War Dove
Troy Cabida

Animal Experiments
Anja Konig

Sylvanian Family
Summer Young

Greenface
Anita Pati

Piano Version
Daisy Thurston-Gent

bloodthirsty for marriage
Susannah Dickey

At the Speed of Dark
Gabriel Àkámọ

Rheuma
William Gee

A Terrible Thing
Gita Ralleigh

TONIPOEM
Victoria Adukwei Bulley

The Tale of the Turkish Carpet
Jacqueline Saphra

2019

While I Yet Live
Gboyega Odubanjo

She Too Is a Sailor
Antonia Jade King

Raft
Anne Gill

And They Are Covered in Gold Light
Amy Acre

Blank
Jake Wild Hall

Alter Egos
Edited by Amy Acre and Jake Wild Hall

The Body You're In
Phoebe Wagner

No Weakeners
Tim Wells

After the Stabbing
Zena Edwards

The Lives of the Female Poets
Clare Pollard

Give Thanks / for Shukri
Amaal Said

South of South East
Belinda Zhawi

2018

In My Arms
Setareh Ebrahimi

The Story Is
Kate B Hall

I'm Shocked
Iris Colomb

Ode to Laura Smith
Aischa Daughtery

The Pale Fox
Katie Metcalfe

TIGER
Rebecca Tamás

The Death of a Clown
Tom Bland

The Dizziness Of Freedom
Edited by Amy Acre and Jake Wild Hall

2017

Solomon's World
Jake Wild Hall

Unremember
Joel Auterson

Lightning Source UK Ltd.
Milton Keynes UK
UKHW010656300920
370782UK00002B/60